The Life File

Created by

Sandy Weatherburn

Social Embers

First Edition Published 2016
This Edition Published 2020

www.socialembers.com

The Life File

CONTENTS

What is The Life File?

A simple way of recording the details of your life efficiently and safely. Where are important documents such as, your will, insurance and pension details kept? If you have a pet, what is the vet's name? These are some of the questions that The Life File can help you answer, by using it to record important details all in one place.

The Life File can be completed at any time to help you organise your life, and can also be amended at any point. There is space in this book to record both practical details and personal and emotional ones, but if you want to create your own personal file based around the information in this book, you are of course free to do so.

Some of the subjects that are included may not be something that you have ever considered. We hope that by including these it will prompt you to give some of these points a bit of thought, and perhaps even discuss them with your partner, friend or relative.

If you choose not to answer some of the questions, because you find the subject too difficult, then leave those parts blank until you do feel that you can complete them.

Keep The Life File in a secure place, but where it can be found easily and tell someone close to you that you have one. We know that not everyone feels comfortable with writing down personal information and we ask that you **DO NOT record your passwords** in The Life File.

More copies of this book can be purchased from **www.socialembers.com**.

The Life File is not a legal document and so should not be considered as a replacement for a Last Will & Testament, Lasting Power of Attorney or an Advance Expression of Wish. It is recommended that everyone makes a legal will, preferably with a solicitor, who can also explain the importance of a Lasting Power of Attorney.

My Personal Details

TITLE	
FORENAME(S)	
LAST NAME	
MAIDEN NAME OR PREVIOUS NAME	
THE NAME I USE (OR NAME I PREFER TO BE KNOWN AS)	
DATE OF BIRTH	
ADDRESS	
TELEPHONE NUMBER	
MOBILE NUMBERS(S)	
EMAIL ADDRESS(ES)	

Emergency Contacts

It is important that you tell the people listed here that they have been included in The Life File as an emergency contact and that you have their permission for someone to contact them in an emergency. It might also be useful to tell them where you keep The Life File.

TITLE	
FULL NAME	
RELATIONSHIP TO YOU	
ADDRESS	
TELEPHONE NUMBER	
MOBILE NUMBER	
EMAIL ADDRESS	
ANY OTHER INFORMATION REGARDING CONTACTS	

PERSON ONE	PERSON TWO

Your Next of Kin

TITLE	
FORENAME(S)	
SURNAME	
RELATIONSHIP TO YOU	
ADDRESS	
HOME PHONE NUMBER	
MOBILE NUMBER	
EMAIL ADDRESS	
ANY OTHER INFORMATION	

Medical Notes

NAME AND ADDRESS OF YOUR DOCTOR
MEDICAL OR NHS NUMBER
DO YOU HAVE ANY ALLERGIES TO MEDICINES
DO YOU HAVE AN ORGAN DONAR CARD OR HAVE YOU OPTED OUT OF ORGAN DONATION

Organ Donation in UK

A new law came into effect in England, UK on the 20th May 2020, known as Max and Keira's law. This means that all adults in England are considered to be an organ donor when they die, unless they have opted out, or are in one of the excluded groups. This change brings England in line with Wales. Scotland plan to adopt a similar law in March 2021, Northern Ireland will review the law position in 2021, but until then, the NHS donor registration system continues. For full information visit www.organdonation.nhs.uk

For other countries, refer to the relevant government or health guidelines.

Families are always consulted before organ donation goes ahead, even with an 'opt out' system. If you feel strongly about this issue, then it is important that you make them aware of your wishes.

If you have private medical insurance, please record the details of the provider and claims contact number below.

Important Documents

Use this form to record the physical location of important documents

Your will is covered in more detail on a later page, so please do not record details of it here.

BIRTH CERTIFICATE
MARRIAGE OR CIVIL PARTNERSHIP CERTIFICATE
PASSPORT
PROPERTY DEEDS
DRIVING LICENCE
INSURANCE POLICIES (HOUSE, CAR, ETC)
DECREE ABSOLUTE (DIVORCE PAPERS)
OTHERS

Business and Employment

EMPLOYER CONTACT DETAILS
IF YOU ARE A SOLE TRADER OR DIRECTOR, RECORD THE COMPANY NAME AND REGISTERED OFFICE DETAILS
SOLICITOR CONTACT DETAILS
ACCOUNTANT CONTACT DETAILS
IF YOU HAVE WEBSITES YOU RUN, PLEASE RECORD THE DETAILS OF THE WEB HOSTING PROVIDER
ANY OTHER INFORMATION

Financial Institutions

Please <u>DO NOT</u> list account numbers, passwords or PIN numbers!

For each bank or building society account, please record the information on the page opposite.

Also include details of any credit cards with an outstanding balance, or loans that you may have.

PROVIDER	Contact Details (if an internet only account, just write "On Line")
MORTGAGE PROVIDER (NAME AND ADDRESS)	

Pension Schemes

Use this form to record the details of any occupational pension schemes you are entitled to receive payments from (or you are already receiving payments from).

For UK residents it will also be useful to record your National Insurance number here.

PROVIDER/COMPANY	Location of last statement and contact information

17

Utilities and Service Providers

ELECTRICITY
GAS
WATER
TELEPHONE
MOBILE PHONE
BROADBAND
TV, e.g. Sky
LANDLORD CONTACT DETAILS
OTHER

Your Pets

TYPE OF PET	
NAME	
GENDER	
YEAR OF BIRTH	
VET NAME AND CONTACT DETAILS	
PET INSURANCE DETAILS (IF ANY)	
WHO WOULD YOU LIKE TO TAKE CARE OF YOUR PET?	
OTHER, e.g. behaviour, characteristics and preferred brand of food	

PET 1	PET 2

Dependants

Use the page opposite to record the details of anyone who relies on you for care; perhaps you are a guardian for a young person, or you have an elderly relative who you care for. Consider providing contact details and any other information you think might be helpful.

Embryology and Fertility Treatment

Following the landmark legal case in 2016 where a mother won the right to use her dead daughter's stored embryos to try to give birth to her own grandchild, we have included a page for recording of any cases of stored embryos eggs or sperm. We appreciate that this page may not be relevant to many, however we feel that it is very important.

If you are undergoing fertility treatment, then you may have sperm, eggs, or embryos stored. You may also have these stored if you are undergoing treatment for cancer.

Use the space opposite to record your wishes as you feel is appropriate to your individual circumstances. You many have recorded this information elsewhere, in which case please record where this information can be found.

You can give consent to the posthumous use of storage of your embryos after your death by your partner, (or your recipient if you are a donor). Valid consent must be in writing and signed before your death, so we have included a space for your signature and date.

My wishes for any stored embryos or sperm.

My Name :

Signed: **Date :**

Your Faith

Do you follow a religion or faith? If you would like others caring for you to know about this, then please record it in the box opposite.

Are you a member of a particular religious community? The details recorded here would allow anyone caring for you to notify that community if you were incapacitated or had died. Please record the address or a contact in the box on the opposite page.

Would you want your religious beliefs taken into consideration by someone organising your funeral? We have left space here for you to record in your own words what is important to you, but there are more specific questions on the My Funeral page.

Funeral Pre-Payment Plan

If you have a pre-paid funeral plan, or an insurance policy to cover the cost of your funeral, please record the details here.

COMPANY NAME
ADDRESS
TELEPHONE NUMBER
EMAIL ADDRESS
WHERE DO YOU KEEP THE DOCUMENTS RELATING TO THIS?

Living Will

What is a living will and why might you need one?

Lasting Power of Attorney (LPA) was previously called Enduring Power of Attorney, this was changed when a new system was introduced, with The Mental Capacity Act 2005. Lasting Power of Attorney is a legal document that gives the named person the authority to make decisions on your behalf if you were mentally incapacitated. There are two different types: one for financial decisions and one for health care decisions.

A living will is different to an LPA and is not a legally binding document, (it is also different to an Advanced Directive or Statement). If you want to record preferences as to how you would like to be cared for, a living will would act as a guide to those providing your care, and may help relatives make decisions on your behalf.

It is important to note that it is the document with the latest date that takes precedence, whether an LPA or a Living Will. If you want to make an Advanced Directive or Statement to refuse treatment, this must be witnessed and signed and we strongly recommend that you discuss this with your solicitor and GP before putting this in place.

We have listed some suggestions, this is not an easy thing to consider when you are fit and healthy, and we understand that you may want to give some time to think about these questions.

You may decide that any decision about your care is best left to the health professionals, and that is fine, but your family may find some of the information listed here useful.

- Where would you prefer to live if you were unable to care for yourself?
- Do you have any dietary preferences, such as vegetarian or vegan?
- What type of music do you like to listen to?
- Do you like being with animals?
- What colour clothes do you like to wear?

Please feel free to add any information that you think is relevant and important to you on the next page.

My Living Will

My Name:

Signed: **Date:**

Will and Lasting Power of Attorney

LOCATION OF YOUR WILL
PLEASE PROVIDE NAME AND CONTACT DETAILS IF HELD AT A SOLICITORS
EXECUTOR(S) (AS LISTED IN YOUR WILL).
PLEASE PROVIDE NAME AND CONTACT DETAILS OF YOUR EXECUTOR(S)
IF YOU HAVE A FINANCIAL OR HEALTH LPA WHERE ARE THEY KEPT?
PLEASE PROVIDE NAME(S) AND CONTACT DETAILS OF THOSE NOMINATED IN ANY LPAS

HEALTH LPA	FINANCIAL LPA

Funeral Wishes

Have you ever been to a funeral and thought about how you would like yours to be? Perhaps not, but the page opposite offers you space to record your wishes for some of the decisions that relatives would have to make for you if they were planning your funeral. You may not want to fill in any of these details, as you trust their judgement, and that too is fine.

We have listed some questions to provoke you to consider the many options available for an end of life ceremony or funeral. Please do not feel you have to answer them all.

- Would you prefer to be buried or cremated? (This decision may be part of your religion or may have a financial impact on your family)
- Have you purchased a burial plot? If so where is it?
- If you prefer to be cremated is there anywhere particular that you would like your ashes to be scattered or interned?
- Would you prefer a natural burial?
- Have you preferences about embalming?
- Are you entitled to a military funeral?
- Would you prefer a wicker or ecological coffin or urn for your ashes?
- What would you like people to wear to your funeral?
- What would you like to be wearing?
- Do you have any preferred music choices that you would like to be played at your funeral? If you have, write them here.
- The same for poetry or readings.
- Would you like your funeral to be recorded (video and/or audio)?
- Have you written your own eulogy? If so where is it kept?
- Who would you like to read your eulogy? Have you discussed this with them?
- Would people be allowed to take photographs at your funeral?
- What would you like people to do after your funeral?
- Would you like flowers at your funeral or would you prefer donations to be given to a charity? If so which charity would you prefer to be chosen?
- Is there anyone who you may not have been in regular contact with, that you think should be told that you had died?

Your Memorial
How would you like to be remembered?

There are many of us who will never give this question a thought, and others who plan for it. You may not want to be remembered at all, or you may want to leave that up to those who are living.

Often the cost of a physical memorial is a big consideration and an addition to funeral expenditure. So if you would like to remembered in a particular way or place, then record that here, but make sure that it is achievable otherwise your family may not be able to carry out your wishes.

Have you recorded a message for family and friends such as a voice recording or video? If you have, where is it kept and how is it accessed?

Life in the digital era means that our digital footprint becomes our digital legacy when we die. It is important that our digital lives are managed appropriately at the end of life, some people choose to have digital memorials, a virtual space where friends and family can visit. This is a service that we offer, please visit our website to find out more. Social media accounts such as Facebook can be memorialised if you have the correct settings in place. If you would like to find out more about this then we recommend our **Digital Legacy Toolkit** which will give you more information about leaving and creating a digital legacy. Please see our website **www.socialembers.com** for more details about obtaining the Toolkit.

An Introduction to Digital Legacy

As our lives become increasingly connected to the internet, considering what happens to our digital on-line life after death is becoming as important as writing a will for your property, money and possessions.

Not identifying your on-line accounts and preparing a digital legacy could cause your beneficiaries difficulties. In addition, your executors will potentially have to expend more time and effort in administering your estate.

Some of the difficulties that can arise from not managing your digital footprint are:

- Identity theft and fraud
- Lack of account access for your executors
- Continuing subscriptions for on-line services
- Lost digital assets (which can have real monetary values)
- On-line memorialisation wishes not carried out

Social Embers enables you to leave a Digital Legacy, as part of writing your will to help your appointed executors.

The Social Embers Digital Legacy Toolkit

We supply you with our Digital Legacy Toolkit, which contains helpful information about on-line accounts and how to record them, as well as guidance on social media account memorialisation and on-line memorials.

Perhaps the most important part of leaving a Digital Legacy is the record of your on-line accounts, so that your executors know about them and are able to take the appropriate action to close them. We have developed a Digital Expression of Wish form, which you can use to easily record details of your digital accounts, along with your wishes for them.

Once completed and signed, the Digital Expression of Wish will be held by your solicitor along with your will.

The Digital Legacy Toolkit includes a checklist for you to complete, to make sure that you have considered all aspects of your digital life when recording your Digital Legacy.

Please visit **www.socialembers.com** for details of the Digital Legacy Toolkit.

. . . And Finally

We have called this book The Life File as it is mostly about your life. When your life ends, relatives and friends are likely to be sad and upset, but completing The Life File, will promote conversations that may not have otherwise been started which will help them in understanding your life and death.

There are so many different scenarios for perfect end of life care, but talking to relatives and recording your personal wishes for your death, only highlights the importance of your life.

Thank you for purchasing The Life File, which has been produced to support the work of Social Embers in raising awareness of end of life issues.

Our email address is **sandy@socialembers.co.uk** if you have any questions or thoughts on this book.

We have included some blank pages at the end of The Life File for any additional notes.

Additional Notes

Additional Notes

Additional Notes

Additional Notes

Additional Notes

Additional Notes

Printed in Great Britain
by Amazon